PRAISE FOR
DON CAMPBELL
AND HIS EARLIER WORKS

*"Don Campbell is one of the great geniuses of our times.
His presentations are high art, involving all the senses
and bringing his audiences to a new level of
insight, delight, creativity, and aliveness."*

— JOAN Z. BORYSENKO, PH.D.,
the author of *Minding the Body, Mending the Mind*

*"Don Campbell's work is a driving force for an emergent field.
The exercises guide one into the rich depth of
consciousness and artistic expression."*

— JEANNE ACHTERBERG,
the author of *Imagery in Healing* and
Woman as Healer

The Harmony of Health

ALSO BY DON CAMPBELL

Books

The Mozart Effect®

The Mozart Effect for Children

100 Ways to Improve Teaching Using Your Voice & Music: Pathways to Accelerate Learning

Music: Physician for Times to Come

Rhythms of Learning: Creative Tools for Developing Lifelong Skills

The Roar of Silence

Music and Miracles

Master Teacher, Nadia Boulanger

Introduction to the Musical Brain

The Magic of Amadeus, Volumes 1–7 (Japanese)

Music CDs

Music for The Mozart Effect, Volumes 1–6 (for Adults)

The Mozart Effect: Music for Babies

The Mozart Effect: Music for Children

The Mozart Effect: Music for Moms & Moms-to-Be
The Mozart Effect: Music for Dads & Dads-to-Be

Spoken Word

The Wisdom and Power of Music

Healing Yourself With Your Own Voice

Mozart as Healer

♪

Please visit Hay House USA: www.hayhouse.com®
Hay House Australia: www.hayhouse.com.au
Hay House UK: www.hayhouse.co.uk
Hay House South Africa: orders@psdprom.co.za
Hay House India: www.hayhouseindia.co.in

The Harmony of Health

Sound Relaxation
for Mind, Body, and Spirit

DON CAMPBELL

HAY HOUSE, INC.
Carlsbad, California
London • Sydney • Johannesburg
Vancouver • Hong Kong • Mumbai

Published and distributed in the United States by: Hay House, Inc.: www.hayhouse.
com • *Published and distributed in Australia by:* Hay House Australia Pty. Ltd.: www.
hayhouse.com.au • *Published and distributed in the United Kingdom by: Hay House
UK, Ltd.: www.hayhouse.co.uk* • *Published and distributed in the Republic of South
Africa by:* Hay House SA (Pty), Ltd.: orders@psdprom.co.za • *Distributed in Canada
by:* Raincoast: www.raincoast.com • *Published in India by:* Hay House Publications
(India) Pvt. Ltd.: www.hayhouseindia.co.in • *Distributed in India by:* Media Star:
booksdivision@mediastar.co.in

Editorial supervision: Jill Kramer • *Design:* Charles McStravick

"The Gang That Sang Heart of My Heart": words and music by Ben Ryan
    © 1926 (renewed) EMI Robbins Catalog, Inc.
All Rights Controlled by EMI Robbins Catalog, Inc. (Publishing) and
Alfred Publishing Co., Inc. (Print)
    All rights reserved. Used with permission.

Library of Congress Control Number: 2005935416

ISBN 13: 978-1-4019-0884-3
ISBN 10: 1-4019-0884-5

09 08 07 06   4 3 2 1
1st printing, April 2006

Printed in the United States of America

I dedicate this book to my Campbell musical lineage:
my father, Forest, who played the piano,
harmonica, organ, or guitar for fun;
my aunts Henrietta, Marguerite, Christine, and Ruby,
who played for the Methodist church,
Eastern Star, and nursing homes;
and my uncle Cleo, who tinkered with the
keyboard and loved to sing along with everyone.

They brought the power of music
to my imagination with great love.

Contents

Foreword

*B*eing the director of a stress-disorder clinic at a Harvard Medical School teaching hospital for nearly a decade, I learned that stress reduction wasn't just for our patients. As staff, we were pressured by time, information overload, and the need to balance work, family, and our inner lives. Just as for all people, learning to manage stress and staying centered was integral to doing our best work and being our best selves. Music is one of the easiest ways to facilitate the shift out of a worried, harried mind to the peaceful, serene center. Knowing this, many of us played classical music as soft background in our offices. It created a field of peace, inspiration, and healing, both for ourselves and for our patients.

A recent worldwide poll showed that music is the most popular way for people to manage stress all over the globe. Teenagers in New Jersey, mothers in Tanzania, and businesspeople in India are all alike in this regard. Music brings them back into the present moment and gives the mind and body a break. Most of the patients in our clinic found that music not only helped them relax, it also helped them focus more easily during meditation. Many also reported that listening to classical or spiritually evocative music through headphones during surgery and chemotherapy was deeply relaxing, comforting, and healing—observations that research has since corroborated.

Don Campbell is, in my view, the world's leading expert on music and the brain. His books, including *The Mozart Effect* and *The Mozart Effect for Children*, detail the effects of music on brain function, creativity, mood, and health. His many audio programs of carefully chosen classical compositions can enhance mood, performance, and healing while reducing stress and tension. When I wrote the book *Inner Peace for Busy People: 52 Simple Strategies for Transforming Your Life,* music was one of those strategies. Don and I decided to create a special CD of classical music together with the same title as the book, and it's still one of my favorite albums for relaxation, inspiration, and enhanced creativity.

As research on the healing power of music has increased, many hospitals have added musical selections to their inpatient television channels, as well as in public spaces. The idea is to create a total-healing environment for patients, visitors, and staff. It's no surprise that Don Campbell is a pioneer in this area. He has worked with a new hospital in Colorado to create a varied program of thousands of musical pieces, which play in changing sequences keyed to time of day, place, and care environment.

Music is vibration. Just as a tuning fork, when struck, can cause other tuning forks in its vicinity to start vibrating at its pitch, music can change your energy. In a practical sense, it can change your brain. And that, in turn, can change every aspect of your life. In this book, Don Campbell shows you how to use this powerful, wondrous, delightful medium to enhance the quality of your life. Relax and enjoy!

— JOAN Z. BORYSENKO, PH.D.,
the author of *Inner Peace for Busy People*
and *Inner Peace for Busy Women*

"Music is not only an art and a refined form of beauty's expression; it is also the subtle and dynamic power that unifies breath, rhythm, and tone of the human body. Every thought, feeling, and movement has its own musical qualities."

◆◆◆ **DON CAMPBELL** ◆◆◆

From *Music: Physician for Times to Come*

Overture

From the beginning of human history, music has served as a tool for expressing our hopes, desires, and pains, for celebrating our triumphs and mourning our losses. Instinctively, we have long understood that music can alter our emotions as well, helping us shake off our darker moods and open the door to peace.

During the past 25 years, research has confirmed what we've always known intuitively: Music can literally help us release our fear, anger, and confusion, and rebalance our minds and bodies. When we feel refreshed and invigorated, the power of health and light begins to radiate from ourselves to the world around us. That inner glow shines through every cell in the body. The energy of sound moving through the air affects our bodies and minds in ways we may scarcely notice, or perhaps simply disregard. Music, a universal language as ancient as time itself, can be used in more diverse and practical ways than we usually acknowledge.

Music, much like food, has nutritional value for our minds and bodies. At times it may be too loud or too heavy for healthy listening, yet the same sounds might energize us in very positive ways on occasion.

During my nine years as director of the Institute for Music, Health, and Education in Boulder, Colorado, I was involved in numerous studies demonstrating music's healing powers. In today's fast-paced world, stress can be one of the most debilitating factors affecting our health. That's why learning to relax in order to alleviate that stress is crucial to our long-term well-being.

This book will enable you to explore some of the most innovative and integrative tools for self-relaxation. This is a practical work that can help you develop relaxation techniques with music, assisted by visual forms and affirmations. My role is to remind you of the wisdom—which you have always possessed on an intuitive level—of combining these tools to relieve your stress.

Music's Power

It's amazing that in just a few minutes, music can trigger responses in your heartbeat, emotions, and attentiveness. Almost instantly, you can be activated, awakened, and feel like dancing.

More than entertainment or just great art, music is a source of physical energy capable of influencing every single cell in your body. It releases chemical responses in the brain that affect the way you feel. Chronic noise and dissonant sounds can create patterns of stress that build up over the years. Increasingly, however, music therapy, music psychology, and psychoacoustics are being used to integrate positive sound into our daily lives. For example:

- Dr. Raymond Bahr, director of a coronary care unit in Baltimore, Maryland, reports his finding that half an hour of music can produce the same effect in a patient as ten milligrams of Valium.

- Researchers in Russia and India have confirmed that plants exposed to music produce better yields.

- Canadian scientists claim that wheat seedlings grow up to three times longer when treated with tones.

- In monasteries in northwest France, monks have experimented with playing music and chanting to their animals. It turns out that cows serenaded with Mozart produced more milk.

- Immigration-department officials in Seattle have begun playing classical and baroque music during English classes for new arrivals from Asian countries. They report that the sounds help release stress and improve the immigrants' language development.

Numerous clinical and long-term studies indicate that clear, orderly music that isn't overstimulating can make a dynamic contribution to your health and wellness. You can begin to explore this world of beauty and stress relief by listening to the selections on the accompanying CD. As you listen, look through the suggestions and the art in this book. In this way, you'll begin using your other senses to integrate the power of sound. As you become a skilled and invigorated listener, you can create your own soundtrack—your own images of relaxation, health, and inspiration.

Using Music as a Vital Tool to Keep Your Mind and Body Refreshed

Music changes our sense of time, how we experience the world around us. It can expand our perceptions and bring clarity to the mind. The auditory structures of harmony, rhythm, and melody affect the rhythms of the body, and the nonverbal language of music can create a vast range of emotions connected to past experiences. A melody may instantly evoke events from earlier parts of our lives, or take us back through the centuries to envision other societies and historical times. It also connects us to the rhythms of our day. Musical qualities are present in every physical movement. The rhythmic quality of the body frames every kinesthetic action. The slower breaths and heartbeats during sleep affect the brain waves and the many cycles of the organs.

By learning to consciously listen to and use music, your daily practice of centering, balancing, and relaxation becomes your own art form. From the simple exercises you'll learn over the next five days, you can create your own visual and resonating repertoire for each day's refreshment. You'll discover that music can prolong your sense of rest and comfort; it can bring you to a spiritual place where you can connect and pray.

We may awaken in the morning with the help of "sonic caffeine" and fall asleep to a "sonic sedative." In between, we might consciously turn to music to block out the world and give us energy and creative power—notice how many people have headphones on as they walk down the street or commute to school or work.

In our modern culture, it's easy to see how sound influences us in other ways that remain outside our awareness. Television and radio programs, musical signals on the train and bus, cell-phone ring tones, and other beeps and buzzes emitted by the machines that surround us affect our moods whether or not we notice them.

As we mature, our brains' responses to music and sound—and our sonic needs—begin to change. Increasingly, we welcome quiet, ordered music. We want our environments to feel healthier and more comfortable for us. But in these quiet times, our inner thoughts, especially negative ones, can become louder than outer sounds. Music, used correctly, can help quiet these damaging voices and order our thoughts.

Not every piece of music is equally effective. Many types—including opera, popular music, and dance rhythms—entertain and inspire us. Yet there are times when they're too emotional or seem too stimulating to bring us to a contented, peaceful place.

Just because a composition is slow and soft doesn't mean that it's necessarily healing. Much music from the New Age genre has little or no form, and this type of ambient expression is useful only to a point. The brain and body love order, especially when it's nonconstricting. In other words, a peaceful structure through music is more often healing than just non-structured sounds.

No matter what your background may be, some of the works by Mozart, Bach, or even a contemporary composer can be used for balance and clarity. The magic of fine music brings us to a place of *stimulated* relaxation, which is ideal for the mind and body. Knowing how to listen to music and remembering to use it when we're stressed, worried, or tired can be of great value.

How to Orchestrate Yourself with This Book

The inner universe offers each of us remarkable powers for improving health, creativity, and focus. Through the simultaneous power of music, images, and affirmation, a new way of creating your own harmony is ready to become a reality.

In five days, this book will guide you through five inspirational musical and visual selections that will open your mind, body, and heart to a receptive and reflective state of awareness. Each day will bring a new inner language of sound, color, and form into focus with a sense of well-being and peace through self-exploration of the body and mind.

I suggest that you take five consecutive days to make the relaxing tour through this book. Get used to the affirmations and become familiar with the music. Learning to gaze for five minutes at the art forms may be new to you, but that will also become familiar with practice.

There are three steps of instruction at the end of each chapter. After your five-day exploration, consider taking five weeks to explore and create your own relaxation program. Using exercise, movement, meditation, and your own special style of listening to music, let these simple and powerful images and sounds lead you into the greatest harmony of your life.

♪

Harmony is a state of ongoing alignment from the inner world to the outer, from the mind to the body, from the spirit to the emotions . . . so this is a visionary guidebook for the integration of your life. In these simple and inspiring chapters, we'll explore the daily pathways for better health and balance in less than a week.

During my work with the Institute for Music, Health, and Education, I noticed how the elements of music could be efficiently used to bring a variety of healthy experiences to the body. The very personal sounding of the voice, known as "toning," can be used to release tension. The voice can activate clarity of mind, and it brings energy to the body. In just three minutes, making a relaxed vowel sound, such as "Ah," modifies the brain waves and brings them into balance.

Relaxation isn't necessarily a passive state of rest; it can also be vibrant, focused, and joyful. Expressive movement to rhythmic music activates energy and releases tension, whether you're a dancer or just an armchair conductor of symphonies. Combining movement with imagery and visualization enhances your ability to handle stress.

Many books contain music, guided imagery, and visualizations. However, none give such explicit opportunities for self-exploration and such a unified healing experience within just a week's time. Each of *The Harmony of Health*'s five chapters is designed to create an awakened, conscious sense of peace. After the initial five days of just five to twenty minutes of listening, looking, and affirming, you'll have created a path for a daily harmonic tune-up.

Your body is your instrument, and as such, it needs to be tuned every day. Each time a violinist or guitarist prepares to play or practice, it's necessary to go through this process. Vocalists know that exercises prepare their voices for optimal performance, and a pianist practices scales to warm up the fingers and focus the mind. To that end, healing isn't just for times of sickness and stress; it's a continual necessity. Each day, exercise, diet, and rest—or the lack of these things—all blend with our multiple responsibilities to make up our current state of health. Music, meditation, and deep listening can enhance the way that your human instrument maintains its harmony. These steps will alleviate stress and change the way you feel forever.

"My heart, which is
so full to overflowing,
has often been solaced
and refreshed by music
when sick and weary."

••• **MARTIN LUTHER** •••

Chapter 1

The Heart of Music

At the heart of relaxation lie both energy and repose. It's a state that is both peaceful and responsive; it's flowing, receiving, and giving at the same time. Music's greatest gift is deep rest. It can instill motivation and open the heart to the inspiration that renews faith. It's the voice of the spirit.

In the most obvious way, we can think of relaxation as a state without stress. Tension, uncenteredness, anger, fear, and pain all create different levels of strain. Stress challenges judgment and sends alarming messages to the body. Sometimes the most positive experience can create a challenging situation. Remember the hectic days before a wedding or the preparation for a long-awaited vacation?

Stress can also be caused by environmental allergies, emotional conflicts, the death of a friend, or financial problems. It's triggered by physical, nutritional, psychological, social, and spiritual causes. In the 21st century, we think of this tension as a part of daily life. From traffic jams to weight management, our society is overwhelmed. Advertisements constantly remind us that we aren't perfect and encourage us to buy our way out of our predicaments with pills, self-improvement classes, and new kinds of exercise and diets.

We often misdiagnose ourselves, thinking that we're frazzled because of our jobs or relationships, yet it could be that we're deeply exhausted and running on an "empty" heart. We may be spiritually challenged and feel that our faith isn't nourishing our lives.

When we're stressed for long periods of time, our

immune system begins to suffer. We sense that energy isn't available for all the things that we need and wish to do. Although a nap, a walk, a concert, or an evening spent in front of the TV may help us realign ourselves momentarily, there are ways to build the power of relaxation into your daily routine.

Opening the Heart with the Ears

I have a friend who recently retired at age 60. Dana had been looking forward to this time in her life for more than a decade, creating long lists of things that she wanted to do. During the last year of her work as an elementary school teacher, however, she found herself growing more and more stressed. Her fear of having too much free time and a reduced income became so great that she lost sleep. She was irritable and felt tired and tense for her last few months on the job. Nevertheless, she was still more relaxed in the classroom—where she felt needed by her students and comfortable within her standard daily rhythm—than she did at home contemplating her future.

Dana adapted fairly well the summer after her retirement, since she'd been in that yearly cycle of summer vacations for 35 years. But once school began without her in the fall, she grew more restless than ever, and she was filled with fear about her future and health. She couldn't relax and accept that this was one of the most positive times of her life.

Take a break now from reading Dana's story. Close your eyes, breathe out deeply, and let your mind flow while you ask yourself, *Where is the tension in my body? What causes stress in my life every single day?* Let your mind rest in these thoughts. There's no need to try to figure them out. Simply observe what comes to mind. . . . Become aware of some of the obvious stress factors in your life that may be similar to Dana's.

My friend was creating anxiety because she'd lost her connection to the rhythm of her life. She'd lost contact with her own heart, and her mind was being taken over by fear. She entertained the idea of going back to teaching as a substitute or taking on a few other part-time jobs so that she'd stay occupied. All of her resolutions were covering up the inner challenge of having time: time to rest, choose her activities, and enjoy the things on her to-do list.

Dana hadn't paused to really listen to her heart, intuition, or soul. The many years of routine teaching had slowly chiseled away that deep connection. Although she was religious, she'd never set aside spiritual time at home, since she always felt too tired or busy.

One day, Dana pulled out a box of some old records that she'd collected in the 1950s and '60s. At the top of a stack of these long-forgotten albums was one that her mother had given her for Christmas more than 40 years ago. It wasn't Dana's favorite, but both of her parents had loved it. She put it on the stereo in her living room, which still had her turntable hooked up to it, and the sounds of Mitch Miller's Sing Along choir filled the room:

"Heart of My Heart," I love that melody.
"Heart of My Heart," brings back a memory.
When we were kids on the corner of the block
We were rough and ready guys
But oh how we could harmonize . . .
"Heart of My Heart"

Listening to these lyrics, Dana began to cry. She sat down on the floor as decades of memories flooded back to her all at once. Not only was this one of her parents' favorite songs, but she remembered singing it over and over as a very young girl. Her tears were filled with joy and sorrow: She missed her dear parents and the way they loved that music, yet she also recalled her own happiness when she used to sing these words. Her heart broke open, and it began to glow. She felt alive again with both pain and pleasure.

My friend played that one song a dozen times that evening, listening to the words more closely and letting herself feel her emotions and spirit. Later, Dana told me that the music—that one song—brought her whole being into an awakened state. The weight of retirement, the years of work, and the dread of the future somehow left her in a short time through the power of its notes.

It's wonderful to know how magical a song can be. The energy it created was Dana's source of transformation. In just a month she began to form a new routine, embark on meaningful activities, and even find an outlet for creating music in her life. She began singing with an ensemble from her local chapter of the Sweet Adelines (an international organization of female barbershop singers). Naturally, "The Gang That Sang Heart of My Heart" was the first song she wanted to sing.

Letting Go of Stress

There are many ways to reduce tension in our lives, but at times we can feel blocked. When we've been in such a cycle for a prolonged period, even the best ideas may not bring us into balance until we experience a release, a moment of great surrender.

Dana helped me realize how important it is to let go of old patterns and activities in order to build a new era of freedom.

Once my friend opened her heart and emotions, the ability to sleep, exercise, and build new friendships came much more easily; and her fears of loneliness and loss began to fade away. This transition wasn't immediate, but she'd truly allowed her heart to soothe her mind with music. Her emotions, thoughts, and body began to have a new relationship with each other, and within a few months she was building a new life. The harmony of health began to grow every day.

Using the CD with Visualizations

Now it's time to take the first steps in building a pathway of harmony from the ears and eyes to the mind and body. At the end of this chapter you'll see a heart, the first of five images that will start you on your inner journey. This picture is very clear—intended not so much as an artistic interpretation as a focal point for your thoughts and feelings.

On the CD at the end of the book, you'll find five tracks of recordings, one for each of the chapters and visualizations herein. Each chapter also includes a simple affirmation, one that you can easily memorize and use without any difficulty.

It would have been so easy for me to simply write about music and have you listen to its beauty. But that wouldn't open the possibilities of harmonic transformation for you. The music itself isn't enough at times. When you enhance the listening process with different visual and mental tools, however, the music can become more powerful.

Using Music, Visualization, and Affirmations for This Chapter

Step One

Affirmation:
Beauty and calmness are forever filling my heart.

This is truly a harmonic idea. Take a few minutes to repeat the affirmation . . . then close your eyes and whisper it to yourself . . . and then think it silently.

Step Two

After the affirmation feels comfortable and spontaneous, look at the heart design at the end of the chapter.

● Sit with the book directly in front of you, with your head lifted (rather than having the book in your lap).

- Say the affirmation a few more times as you look directly into the middle of the heart. See if you can keep your eyes focused right in the center as you inhale.

- Hold your breath for a few seconds, then breathe out the affirmation. Do this five or six times as you keep your eyes centered on the heart.

- Close your eyes and rest in the thought and image. Notice that you can see the heart with your inner vision.

Step Three

Play Track 1 of the enclosed CD. This is a heart-centered piece called "Beloved" by Michael Hoppé (available on the Spring Hill Music album *Solace*).

- Listen to the selection once with your eyes closed with the intent of opening *your* heart. Then play the piece again as you look into the center of the heart figure.

- Repeat this affirmation: *Beauty and calmness are forever filling my heart.* . . . Let your eyes, ears, and mind feel the attunement of this powerful exercise.

- Finally, rest and notice your body . . . does it feel calm?

There are many ways to use this exercise. You may want to take your time and spend a whole week on the heart, letting the haunting melody flow through your daily life. You may wish to keep the heart image in your mind and see how many times each day you can see and feel its power, or you might experiment with the affirmation at times when you feel stress.

Let the exercise flow naturally. Enjoy the music and let your heart be your foundation. Whether you read a chapter a day or spend five days on each one, just remember to check in with your feelings. Allow yourself to take the most relaxed path you can to explore your natural potential.

*Beauty and calmness
are forever filling my heart.*

Music: Track 1, "Beloved" from *Solace,*
by Michael Hoppé

"*Music washes away*
from the soul
the dust of everyday life."

••• SIR THOMAS BEECHAM •••

Chapter 2

The Sphere of Harmony

*S*tories illustrating music's power to reduce stress have been told and retold for thousands of years. For example, the Bible tells of David, the giant-slayer, whose lovely harp playing soothed the anxieties of the powerful King Saul.

From Greece to China, music was a bridge of magic for spiritual and physical transformation. Pythagoras's two-stringed monochord provided the basis for all future tuning and mathematical correlations to sound.

Plato sensed the power of the musical interval for creating war, harmony, or cures. In China, intervals and tones served identical purposes through the use of bells, chimes, and gongs. Even Bach was commissioned to compose *The Goldberg Variations* to help one of his wealthy patrons fall asleep.

A few years ago, I gave a series of lectures on the healthful aspects of music to the subscribers of the Cincinnati Symphony Orchestra. During one of the question-and-answer sessions, a lovely lady mentioned that she and her husband had attended the Friday-evening concerts for more than 30 years . . . and throughout every one of those events, her husband had fallen asleep during the first half hour. She found it frustrating and embarrassing, and she wanted to know what she could do to help him pay attention and reap the benefits of the music.

The woman's husband, who was sitting next to her, blushed, and simply explained that after his workweek, he looked forward to the symphony because it relaxed him. He was able to forget the stress of his job and became renewed by the end of the evening. He felt that the second half of each performance was the high point of his week. His wife then understood that music was having a deeper impact on his life than she realized.

From my earliest days as a health-conscious musician, I began to experiment with composing music to help others relax. By integrating low, prolonged thematic phrases based on breathing patterns with higher, superimposed rhythmic harmonies, I found that I could actually write music that spoke to different parts of the mind and body. The higher sounds allowed beautiful mental images to form, while the lower sounds set up long phrases that affected breathing. A dynamic change in the depth or shallowness of breath became apparent within three to seven minutes of listening.

The result was *Crystal Meditations,* an album that was used in many of the studies for relaxation at the University of Texas Southwestern Medical Center in Dallas, under the observation of Jeanne Achterberg, Ph.D. Most of the patients in these studies suffered from stress, anxiety, high blood pressure, and lack of concentration.

However, the results of this multilayered music were easily observed in the changes in patients' brain waves, blood pressure, heartbeats, and breathing patterns. Even I was surprised to see that it took only seven minutes of listening for each patient to enter a measurably calmer state of being.

For the first time in my career as a composer, I began to look at the body as a kind of instrument itself—one capable of achieving a resonant state with the power of sound. By that time in my career, I'd written scores for modern-ballet companies and had seen how effectively music directed the movement and expression of the dancers. I began to search for additional compositional techniques that would bring alignment to non-dancers. At the same time, I started experimenting with combining imagery and music in order to access the other senses' potential for sparking the dramatic physical responses that can lead to daily self-improvement.

I gave a cassette of what I'd composed for the hospital studies to my 80-year-old mother. Her response, although a little startling, displayed some insight as well: "I can't believe that your father and I sent you to the conservatory in Fontainebleau, and this is what you're creating. It makes me want to fall asleep!"

For someone like my mother, who was high-strung and very physically tense, this music was actually having a physical effect. She didn't consider it art or entertainment; it was a sedative. Little did she know that that effect was precisely what I'd intended.

Harmonic Massages

The past two decades have brought music's power into hospitals, rehabilitation centers, assisted-living facilities, dental offices, massage rooms, spas, and exercise classes. Highly clinical work on head injuries, strokes, and autism is now performed by certified music therapists, and relaxation techniques are commonly used by psychotherapists. Music provides an essential tool to improve the effectiveness of these professionals.

Massage therapists are able to bring added value to their sessions by using progressive-music-relaxation techniques during each massage. "With many clients, the right music helps set the atmosphere and lets me do my work more deeply and effectively. Not only does it help my clients relax more quickly, the music at the end of the session helps them center and become more grounded and integrated as I massage their feet," says Bev Sharette, a longtime massage therapist in Boulder, Colorado. "Silence is also important. As I get to know each client, I can tune in to their musical preferences."

Many of my students have used a three-phase system of music for massage sessions:

1. Induction, comfort, and release
   for 20 minutes

2. Deep relaxation and surrender
   for 20 minutes

3. Centering, integration, and grounding
   for 5 to 10 minutes

A wide variety of music is used in each of the three phases, depending on the client's physical and psychological needs. Classical selections, New Age music, light jazz, inspirational hymns, and chant all fit into the menu. There are even pieces that help the therapist maintain stamina and strength for the last clients of the day.

The Pillow That Heals

Last year I became aware of research being done in Europe with a pillow that heals. As the director of music and acoustic services with Aesthetic Audio Systems, my interest in bringing music to health-service environments has greatly increased as the medical community has come to accept the arts as a more vital part of treatment. It had long been clear to me that not only would a better acoustic environment benefit patients; but that the medical staff, visitors, and families required a healthier and safer acoustical environment as well.

During my research into this topic, my associate

Annette Ridenour brought to my attention a curative pillow designed in Denmark by the composer Niels Eje and physician Per Thorgaard. These collaborators' belief in the positive effect of music in a clinical setting is so strong that they've created one of the world's largest foundations to study its benefits. The pillow they designed, already thoroughly studied in Europe and now employed in pilot programs throughout the United States, is used to supplement traditional treatments for patients during the high-stress periods immediately preceding and following surgery. Speakers imbedded in the comfortable cushion play recorded natural sounds and soft improvised music, delivering healing melodies directly to the patient without the need for long cords, bulky equipment, or headphones. Patients find the music comforting, but beyond that, studies have shown that using the device reduces their need for preoperative sedation and shortens their postoperative recovery time.

The pillow is just one of many emerging ways that music can assist patients and allow health professionals to do their jobs efficiently. From emergency waiting rooms to maternity wards and operating rooms, stress is an unavoidable part of the health-care experience. Calming the mind and spirit can go a long way toward relaxing and even healing the body. By bringing harmony and accord to the environment—with carefully selected sounds that clarify without overstimulating—all our sensory abilities can be brought together to improve our emotional outlook, resolve, and physical strength.

Optimizing the Power of Relaxation

Studies have shown that prolonged periods of stress create wear and tear on the body. The immune system is suppressed, increasing the chances of hypertension, headaches, stroke, coronary artery disease, and high blood pressure. Simple techniques can be used daily, however, to lessen the tension that can lead to these and other complications. For nearly three decades, psychologists and mind-body therapists have made use of these progressive-relaxation techniques to heal their patients.

This simplified version is designed to consume a minimal amount of time and can be accomplished easily in a comfortable chair, lying in bed, or even at work. Take some time to observe its effects, and experiment with adapting it to your own needs.

Progressive Relaxation in Five Minutes

- Find a comfortable position in a chair, on the floor, or in bed.

- Close your eyes and become aware of your breath. Exhale deeply and slowly three or four times.

- As you continue to breathe, release all the tension in your feet and legs. Let them feel light.

- Then release any tightness from your thighs, hips, and pelvis . . . let go of the muscle constriction in the lower parts of the body.

- Imagine all stress leaving your torso, from the depths of your stomach up through your chest.

- Feel a lightness in your shoulders, arms, and hands. Stretch slightly and then let go, sensing greater relaxation coming to your body.

- Release the muscles in your neck, throat, and jaw. Feel the inhaling breath bringing a soothing sensation to these areas.

- Exhale all stress out from your face and the top of your head, allowing your mind to become clear . . . let the breath take away all your thoughts.

- Remain quiet for another minute or two and allow your body to bring itself into balance.

- Exhale with a long breath and begin to stretch, letting your voice sound "Aaaahhhhh."

- Become aware of the room around you, take your time standing up, and then continue your day.

There are many variations on this technique. If you use it at night, it can increase the restfulness of your sleep. It can help you in preparations for meditation or tasks that make you feel stressed. You may even find it useful to perform these exercises before going for a run or starting some other workout.

Music can be used to assist in this process. As you become familiar with the exercises in this book, you can create your own musical style for morning, afternoon, and evening routines. No matter how many times you use this exercise, you'll find that it always provides benefits.

Once you begin to experiment with the progressive-relaxation technique, you may notice more sounds in your environment. Air conditioners, heaters, refrigerators, lights, computers, and traffic all produce noise that you've become so accustomed to that you may not realize how much stress it's creating. If you begin picking up on these disturbances, especially those of low frequency, you may be pinpointing one of the invisible causes of stress.

Some sounds are negatively charged, bringing fatigue and stress to the body. Others can actually charge the brain and body, and create energy and refreshment. Sounds and music are like our diets. We need a balance of silence, stimulation, and relaxation throughout the day; otherwise, our bodies begin to tire.

Using Music, Visualization, and Affirmations for This Chapter

In our exercise for this chapter, we'll visualize ourselves surrounded by harmony, beauty, and well-being.

Step One

Affirmation:
Restfulness and radiance surround my mind and body.

- Close your eyes and begin to sense a large sphere of light and protection around you.

- Take a few minutes to repeat the affirmation; imagine you are in a pleasant bubble of light.

- Relax any part of your body that seems tense and allow your breath to become deeper.

Step Two

After the affirmation feels comfortable and spontaneous, open your eyes and look at the circle image at the end of the chapter.

- Sit with the book directly in front of you with your head lifted (rather than having the book in your lap).

- Say the affirmation a few more times as you look directly into the middle of the circle.

- Keep your eyes focused on the center as you inhale, then breathe out the affirmation.

- Do this five or six times as you keep your eyes centered on the circle.

- Close your eyes and rest in the thought and image. . . . Notice whether you can see the circle with your inner vision.

Step Three

Now begin to play Track 2 of the enclosed CD, which is a pastoral piece called "Sicilienne" by Gabriel Fauré (available on Spring Hill Music's album *Inner Peace for Busy People,* which was inspired by Joan Borysenko's book of the same title).

- Listen to the selection once with your eyes closed with the intention of feeling surrounded with safety.

- Then play the piece again as you look into the center of the circle, feeling the power of the music.

- Next, add this affirmation: *Restfulness and radiance surround my mind and body.*

- Let your eyes, ears, and mind feel the attunement of this beautiful exercise.

- When the music ends, sit and sense the sphere around you and the circle in front of you.

- Take a few breaths and notice the strength that you feel before moving back into the world . . . let it continue to be a place where you can return and rest in the future.

*Restfulness and radiance
surround my mind and body.*

Music: Track 2, "Sicilienne," by Gabriel Fauré

"*Imagination
is not the
talent of some men,
it is the health
of everyone.*"

••• RALPH WALDO EMERSON •••

Chapter 3

Sound Reflections

*E*dmund Jacobson, the scientist and researcher who developed the progressive muscular relaxation technique outlined previously, became so fascinated by this demonstration of the mind-body relationship that he devoted himself to exploring the topic further in the decades that followed his initial work.

In later studies conducted at the University of Chicago, Cornell University, and Harvard University, it was discovered that not only does the mind respond to physical relaxation, but the body responds physically to mental images, too. Participants were asked to imagine walking through a beautiful outdoor environment. When they did so, biofeedback readings indicated that they produced electrical signals in the walking muscles of the legs, even though they were lying down. Results were similar when subjects were asked to imagine running, eating a certain food, or stretching.

You're probably already familiar with this phenomenon in your own life. We all feel certain sensations that don't match our physical experience, such as what occurs when we're asleep. Have you ever dreamed of petting a cat, walking in a forest, or tasting food? These images create the feeling of the experience without it actually happening in the outer world. Let's try a simple exercise to demonstrate the power of this mind-body connection:

- Close your eyes and conjure up the smell of freshly baked bread. Then see all the different kinds of loaves in the store.

> Imagine eating a hot slice with melting butter. . . . Take a couple of minutes to savor this experience.

- Was that delicious? Did the exercise make your mouth water? Could you really smell bread baking?

The body and mind respond to images, whether they're in the imagination or the real world. As the brain orchestrates all the information that it receives from our senses, it creates a full assessment of our situation that allows us to navigate and make judgments. In this way, the vast sensory resources from our unique life experiences are continually influencing the way we live. Great thinkers from Plato to Carl Jung have written about the power of images to spark the unconscious driving forces of our personalities. Music can help amplify these effects, organize our thoughts and sensations, and prolong our state of awareness and self-discovery.

The Mind's Eye and Ear

Jeanne Achterberg, Ph.D., and Frank Lawless, Ph.D., were pioneers in researching the positive effects of imagery and music on the immune system. They found that music is a primary tool for alleviating anxiety and pain during medical procedures because it helps focus the mind and gives a sense of controlled relaxation to the patients. An innovative program at the University of Massachusetts Memorial Medical Center, developed by Jon Kabat-Zinn, Ph.D., found that harp music offers a safe alternative to tranquilizers and mood-modifying drugs.

As a result of many observations such as this and the emergence of the new field of psychoneuro-immunology, medical professionals are beginning to incorporate imagery techniques—including muscular relaxation, visualization, and the use of music—into their practices. Norman Shealy, M.D., who works with pain and health rehabilitation in his clinic in Springfield, Missouri, reports that these combined techniques are "the single most important therapy that we can offer to people with stress and chronic pain."

The body responds in the short term to such clear, organized sensations by increasing its production of endorphins, which are natural opiates, thus elevating mood and providing quick, safe relief from pain and discomfort. Listening to music for five to seven minutes while imagining yourself in a calm, pastel-colored room with beautiful art and furnishings can lead to significant positive changes in your pulse and breathing patterns. Brain-wave rhythms, skin temperature, and blood pressure can all be modified. Over time, as lifelong patterns of stress are *retrained* through music and imagery, increased T-cell levels in the immune system may lead to a long-term improvement in health and well-being.

This combination of sound and inner sight can do more than just improve our health, however. The powerful connection between body and mind—between the senses and the imagination—can affect other aspects of our lives as well. We often talk to ourselves so much that we don't listen to what our physical self wants to tell us.

Music serves to quiet our inner chatter, organizing and clarifying our thoughts and emotions. It allows us to enter a state of deep listening. When we relax into soothing melodies, we deepen our ability to be inspired. We're able to consider and then rehearse challenging events that the future might bring.

Therapists have also found that relaxed states induced with the aid of programmed classical works serve as a profound tool for accessing unexplored areas of the psyche. Music therapist Helen Bonny, whose Guided Imagery and Music system (GIM) remains one of the most thoroughly researched and useful therapeutic methods, has long considered classical music to be a safe and powerful means for "reaching and exploring non-ordinary levels of human consciousness."

By playing the enclosed CD with the intention of just daydreaming and allowing images to arise, you can sense some of music's power. Once you've reached a relaxed, free-flowing state, turn to this book and focus on its simple visual forms and colors. Often, after a few days of following this routine of relaxation and harmonization of the senses, you'll begin to experience interesting new ideas or unusually vivid dreams. While these exercises don't constitute the therapeutic process as used in GIM sessions, they should provide you with an idea of the riches lying dormant within your unconscious mind, waiting to be revealed by visualization and music.

The Sound Around

As you experimented with the techniques I've described, you may have been distracted by the environment around you. Your brain may have had to divert some of its energy to filter out noises from microwaves, televisions, radiators, or telephones. Such ambient sounds can not only distract you while you're attempting to focus on your inner self, they can actually be destructive to the body.

Noise can keep us from feeling relaxed; it can make it difficult to go to sleep and result in being tired rather than refreshed in the morning. We have to "tune out" automatically whether we're on the subway, in the car, or next to an air conditioner. The racket around you—however subtle—may keep you from thinking well without your even being aware of the source of your distraction.

Take a few minutes to assess your home and work environments, thinking of your whole body as an ear. Go to the three rooms in your home where you spend the most time, stand with your eyes closed, and listen. Are there clocks, furnaces, hot-water heaters, or refrigerators singing their frequencies aloud? Is the halogen lamp buzzing? Even from one room to the next, the conditions can be significantly different. Take note of your bedroom: Is it quieter on one side of the room than the other? Do you hear running water or the alarm clock? All of these create an invisible feeling of tension that can affect the way you sleep and relax.

Even sounds at the edge of our perception can have a physical and emotional effect. I've noticed that in a particular section of one of the major-airline lounges at Los Angeles International Airport, a loud, low hum overwhelms the body, even though its frequency is so muted that most people never hear it. I've often watched travelers sit in that area, only to leave after a few minutes, as though fleeing a bad smell. In fact, when I sit in that part of the lounge myself, I feel the noise in my body as an awkward, almost silent discomfort. It creates stress, although most people fail to identify the source of their irritation.

On the other hand, some sounds can help reduce stress in an environment. Birdsong, rippling water, and even a gentle breeze can create a balancing effect in an acoustically dead room. Such tones improve most people's moods and impart a sense of well-being, but for those with sensitive hearing, even these "sound adornments" can cause tension. For example, children with attention deficit disorder are often distracted by every sound. They're unable to complete a simple task because of the sonic interruption.

Some environments need help masking and covering unwanted noise, while other places may benefit from a constant rhythmic pattern to keep energy flowing. Popular music often serves this purpose by energizing a restaurant or place of business. Serving as temporary sonic caffeine, the tunes provide a helpful boost—but extended exposure to either loud or fast music weakens the body.

The element of control over the source of noise is critical. This is obvious when a loud television or stereo in a neighbor's apartment awakens you in the middle of the night. But strangely enough, stress can also be experienced when someone cracks their knuckles in a quiet room or constantly taps their fingernails on a desk. Even the best music can turn into "noise" if the listener isn't able to control it. In this case, *noise* is defined as "unwanted sound." Something may be perceived in this way when it's considered inappropriate and without purpose for extensive periods or at an overly intrusive volume.

At the Maryland Psychiatric Research Center in Baltimore, a number of volunteer subjects were exposed to random noise over a period of days. At the end of this period, they reported feelings of helplessness, tension, unhappiness, anxiety, stress, loss of control, and an inability to sleep. Physical responses included increased levels of sympathetic nervous-system activity and other physiological disorders.

In a study at the University of Mississippi, 60 male undergraduates volunteered to be tested for the effects of loud sound, while others were subjected to average noise levels. The subjects exposed to loud noise showed increased tension, and at times, aggressive behavior.

The long-term negative effects of noise in the environment are legion. Natural hearing abilities begin to decrease, and the body is overcome by inexplicable stress, anxiety, and fatigue. Often depression, midlife crises, or problems during menopause can arise simply from the isolation and loneliness that occur from losing, ever so slightly, the high range of auditory stimulation.

In keeping a healthy mind and body, it's vital to be conscious of, and control, our auditory environment. We should also maintain an awareness of positive sounds that lift our mood. Once our home, work, and other surroundings are improved in this way, we can more effectively orchestrate sonic, visual, and other sensory tools to build a constant communication between body and mind.

Redecorating Your Inner World

By combining visualization with sound and other sensory stimulation, we tap in to our inner reality, the language of emotions and feeling, which feed the endless flow of the imagination. Sometimes the imagery that emerges is deeply symbolic, seeming to come out of nowhere in dreams. At other times, insights present themselves very consciously during focused moments of contemplation. Then there's the moment of magic when we're least expecting a solution, and new ideas seem to fall from the sky.

Our bodies won't always respond in the same ways to the same stimuli: They may react with physical sensations at one time, and with extreme emotions at another. Sometimes when listening to evocative music, vibrant visual pictures come to mind; at others, just a thought emerges, or even a long-buried memory.

No combination of images, sounds, scents, textures, and other forms of stimulation could comprise the only "correct" method. Whether you choose to include meditation, prayer, biofeedback, or visualization in your daily routine, you can use fairly simple techniques to alter fatigue or more complicated states of pain. Even three or four minutes of visualization with music, performed three times a day, can accomplish the practical task of minimizing discomfort from headaches, muscle tension, and inflammation. With practice and experimentation, you can find the combinations that will work best for you.

Imagery and Visualization

Often these two words are confused in their meaning and use. *Imagery* is inclusive of all the senses. The sensations of smell, taste, touch, sound, and sight—whether immediate, recalled, or simply imagined—blend together to create our experiences with imagery.

Visualization, on the other hand, involves the use of a specific image that presents a form or scene to the mind's eye. To look at the simple shapes at the end of each chapter is the most basic type of this technique. The contrast of the pictures with their background colors gives us a pathway for focus, stillness, and relaxation. As opposed to more complex visualizations—such as natural scenes, people, or familiar environments—the geometric forms in this book steady our minds with simplicity and set the stage for the music and affirmation to empower our state of relaxation.

Using Music, Visualization, and Affirmations for This Chapter

Step One

Affirmation:
I am in harmony with the world around me.

Close your eyes and imagine that you're standing in a triangle of fresh air. You're firm and grounded, and feel solid strength in your feet.

- Whether you're sitting or standing, let the earth below support you.

- Take a few minutes to repeat the affirmation.

- Imagine that you're receiving calm and gentle peace. Relax any part of your body that seems tense, and allow your breath to become deeper and more relaxed.

Step Two

After the affirmation feels comfortable and spon-taneous, open your eyes and look at the triangle at the end of the chapter.

- Look at the image with the book directly in front of you, with your head lifted.

- Say the affirmation a few more times as you look directly at the middle of the triangle.

- See if you can keep your eyes focused on the center as you inhale, then breathe out the affirmation.

- Do this five or six times as you keep your eyes centered on the image.

- Finally, close your eyes and rest in the thought and image. Notice whether you can see the triangle with your inner vision.

Step Three

Now begin to play Track 3 of the enclosed CD. This familiar pastoral piece called "Morning," by Edvard Grieg, easily conveys the awakening of a day, with its fresh and radiant glow.

- Fill the triangle around your body with the energy of the sunrise.

- Listen to the selection once with your eyes closed, with the intention of feeling solid, strong, and fresh.

- Then play the piece again as you look into the center of the triangle image at the end of this chapter, feeling the powers of the music surrounding you with natural beauty.

- Say this affirmation: *I am in harmony with the world around me.*

- Close your eyes and let the firm support of the earth calm and relax your body. The triangle can protect your energy and serve as a constant sunrise of balance for your body and mind.

I am in harmony
with the world around me.

Music: Track 3, "Morning" "
from *Peer Gynt Suite No. 1,* by Edvard Grieg

"One good thing
about music,
when it hits,
you feel
no pain."

••• BOB MARLEY •••

Chapter 4

The Body of Music

As a child, my body responded to every sound, and music danced in every cell. I choreographed everything I heard—from "Humpty Dumpty" to *South Pacific,* I sang every tune and danced with imaginary partners. In church, the organ and choir brought colors and images of angels to my four-year-old mind. My body was an ear, and I was perplexed that everyone else wasn't moving as I was.

By the time I was six, I'd been trained to sit still and

57

listen, but it seemed boring to lock up my body when so many glorious things were happening as I heard music. My dad played the piano, accordion, harmonica, and guitar . . . and these instruments were magical. I loved to take the wooden covering off the bottom of the spinet piano, just above the pedals. I could make such exciting tones and see so many colors when I played on the strings while sitting on the pedals.

My grandmother convinced me to make sounds properly by sitting on the bench and playing the patterns of the black and white notes with my fingers. I learned the names of the keys; practiced steady rhythms; and began to translate those lines, spaces, and circles with "arms" into melodies. Within a few years, I'd begun to play music—and to forget the radiant colors and powerful energy that sound had created throughout my body.

Throughout the following decade, my mind remained in control of my auditory experiences. Singing in the choir, playing the clarinet, and studying piano had become a part of every week. At age 13, I entered the American Conservatory of Music in Fontainebleau, France. Within another decade, I'd finished my studies in music education, organ, and conducting, and I accepted my first position as a music teacher.

Nothing had prepared me for the revelations of my initial hour with 30 first graders from 15 countries. You see, I was teaching at an international school in Tokyo where many of the young students didn't speak English. Within the first ten minutes, I realized that my formal education would be useless in helping me organize the tornado-like energy in these children. As I played and sang, they moved, whirled, jumped, and found new ways to use the floor, chairs, and instruments in the classroom.

Those first chaotic weeks with my students were revolutionary, as they taught me to speak in rhythm and rhyme. Their constant movement reflected the harmony and beat of the music, and I soon realized that *high, low, soft,* and *loud* were movements as well as sounds. My students taught me to remember my own vibrant childhood when everything was color and energy.

During my seven years in Japan, I didn't have the same resources that were available to my American and European counterparts. I was being fully reeducated by the children themselves to listen with my body, heart, and intuition. This was the beginning of an important period in my professional life when I began to consider how to integrate imagination into the musical experience.

Throughout the following decade, my interest in the brain, consciousness, and the role of music in health began to mature, enhanced by my additional studies in psychology. Music as therapy and as a healing tool became my focus as I explored the ancient systems of tuning and performance in Greece and India.

Upon reflection, I now realize that at this critical time in my life, I was fortunate to have been given the opportunity to feel music beyond its definitions of art into a more holistic sense . . . of the physical body, spiritual heart, and universal dance.

Expanding Consciousness with Music

In recent decades, our understanding of the relationship between music and consciousness has expanded and matured through the research of psychologists. In the groundbreaking book *The Highest State of Consciousness,* Stanley Krippner describes how music can assist individuals in moving through levels of awareness. From the normal, relaxed waking state, it brings to life an expanded sensory threshold and can evoke daydreaming, trance, meditative conditions, and even rapture.

During these phases of consciousness, our perception of time is modified. With slow-moving and richly textured music, our reliance on left-brain concepts (such as minutes and hours) fades. Time becomes more experiential, based on our memories and emotions. As in our dreams, we can observe many events in detail in a short period of time. With the body deeply relaxed, fear, pain, and anxiety diminish, and images of past experiences emerge with the music.

The music and exercises in this book haven't been chosen for deep therapy, but they *are* designed to give you keys to unlock many of the normal tensions of daily life. The goal is to empower you with visual, auditory, and linguistic tools to ease relaxation.

Choreographing the Body

Psychologists and other therapists have long made use of music's power to access the mind in all its layers and manifestations. Nonverbal activities such as singing, drumming, or playing a musical instrument are now routinely used in clinical settings to regulate patients' emotional, physiological, and social behavior. By simply having people listen to a melody, a music therapist can bring them to an open state of readiness and create a bridge of communication with them. It isn't necessary for them to know music or how to play an instrument, and it isn't the aim of a therapist to teach these skills. Rather, the rhythms, tones, and energy of the tunes are used to create a direct connection to the heart, body, and mind.

Music therapy has developed into a clinical, behavioral science that can modify emotional, physiological, and social behavior. Involving a patient in nonverbal musical activities can make these changes. At other times, just listening to the right harmonies may provide psychological results. These techniques involve a process of interaction between the therapist and the patient, but it doesn't aim to teach music, or even insist that anyone know much about the subject.

In 1983, the National Association for Music Therapy (NAMT) defined its members as specialists using music in the service of persons with needs in mental and physical health, habilitation, rehabilitation, or special education: "The purpose is to help individuals attain and maintain their maximum levels of functioning."

Forms of music therapy sanctioned by the American Music Therapy Association (which now includes the former NAMT) have helped countless thousands of patients improve their functioning in the areas of physical and mental health, rehabilitation, and special education. But music is increasingly used as a tool in other therapeutic fields as well. Chanting, toning, and visualization with music are now routine in alternative medical practices such as acupuncture, chiropractic, and massage for stress reduction and relaxation.

Music has also been shown to regulate work rhythms and improve the tenor of the working day. A 1995 study published in the *Journal of the American Medical Association* that focused on 50 surgeons at the State University of New York at Buffalo found that music lowered the surgeons' blood pressure while operating, enabling them to complete their tasks more accurately and efficiently. While 46 of the surgeons claimed that they worked best while listening to classical music, 2 preferred jazz, and 2 found Irish folk music most useful.

Studies are currently being conducted at Exempla Good Samaritan Hospital in Colorado on the advantages of allowing the entire hospital staff to work accompanied by a variety of classical, jazz, and other relaxing music during the day. And soothing melodies have become a complementary tool for those outside the medical fields as well. Thousands of studies have shown that it enhances performance, health, and memory, no matter what our line of work.

Barbara Crowe's *Music and Soulmaking* remains one of the most thorough and up-to-date books on the expanded use of music to enhance health, productivity, and happiness. There's a list of suggested readings at the end of this book (pages 91–92), including several that describe the healing and spiritual powers of music therapy.

These harmonic sounds are a perfect complement for medical environments. They shouldn't replace the wisdom of a doctor's advice, but they can be a fine assistant in helping you maintain your spirit, creativity, and immune system during times of challenge.

♪

The Benefits of Music for Mind and Body

Music also:

- Aids long-term memory. By listening to tunes and singing songs from our childhood and youth, as well as moving and dancing to the sounds of our early adulthood, we can connect our minds, bodies, and feelings to parts of the brain that can energize and awaken us. Putting new ideas and information into a musical pattern makes them easier to remember.

- Helps maintain strength in both the upper and lower parts of the body, and improves mobility and range of motion. By moving, playing a rhythmic instrument, clapping, and even tapping our feet, we can maintain and enhance motor control of our bodies.

- Contributes to keeping the mind clear.

- Reduces mental and physical stress and anxiety. In just a few minutes, music can assist in the release of tension and keep the emotions in harmony.

- Helps us pass the time when we're worried, lonely, or depressed. Learning to visualize, use affirmations, and listen to music in these situations repatterns our consciousness toward a lighter, more positive peace of mind.

- Motivates us to be creative and think in new ways. Use the music on the accompanying CD as you draw, paint, or write poems.

Apollo was recognized in ancient Greece as the god of both music and medicine, and earthly harmony was regarded as a reflection of celestial balance and resonance. From time immemorial, simple chords and songs have summoned the powers of the invisible and rectified imbalance in the soul. Novalis, a poet and philosopher of the Romantic period, wrote: "Each illness has a musical solution. The shorter and more complete the solution, the greater the music talent of the physician."

Perhaps Novalis was giving us good advice about how we can be our own caregivers—whether we're just watching our breath, noticing the tension in our body, or riding the waves of emotion. Music is a great medicine: Digest it with your heart, listen to it with your soul, and sense the symphony of life itself. All is well.

Using Music, Visualization, and Affirmations for this Chapter

Step One

Affirmation:
I stand in balance, clarity, and beauty.

- Close your eyes and begin to sense that you're standing on a large silver crescent of light.

- Your feet are perfectly able to balance your weight within this beautiful waxing moon.

- Take a few minutes to repeat this affirmation: *I stand in balance, clarity, and beauty.*

- Now imagine that you're standing within a beautiful bowl of light.

- Relax any part of your body that seems tense, and allow your breath to become deeper.

- If it's helpful, stand up as you hold the image within and speak the affirmation.

Step Two

After the affirmation feels comfortable and spontaneous, open your eyes and look at the crescent image at the end of the chapter.

- Sit or stand with the book directly in front of you, with your head lifted, as you repeat the affirmation.

- See if you can keep your eyes focused on the center of the shape as you inhale, then breathe out the affirmation. Do this five or six times.

- Close your eyes and rest in the thought and image. Notice whether you can see the moon shape with your inner vision.

Step Three

Begin to play Track 4 of the enclosed CD: "Andante" from Mozart's *Piano Concerto No. 14 in E Flat Major.*

- Listen to the selection once with your eyes closed, with the intention of balancing your physical body.

- Play the piece again as you look into the center of the crescent, feeling the power of the music surrounding you.

- Next, add this affirmation: *I stand in balance, clarity, and beauty.*

- Let your eyes, ears, and mind pick up the attunement of this physical and mental exercise.

- When the music finishes, feel the sensation of the crescent beneath your feet. Let it continue to be a place where you easily and safely return.

I stand in balance, clarity, and beauty.

Music: Track 4, "Andante"
from *Piano Concerto No. 14 in E Flat Major,* by Mozart

"*Music melts
all the separate parts of
our bodies together.*"

••• ANAÏS NIN •••

Chapter **5**

Harmony of Health

$\mathcal{I}$ncreasingly, music has begun to serve as a common tongue for communication through-out the world. African, Latin, and European sounds have been integrated into much of our own day-to-day songs; and it no longer seems strange to hear Indian, Chinese, and even Tibetan instruments and musical styles in films and concert halls. Today, we easily recognize that all cultures have something to offer from their own traditions.

During my years in graduate school, I became fascinated by India's centuries-old practice of integrating the fluctuating energies of daily life into its music. With more than 4,000 scales and nearly as many rhythmic patterns, Indian composers have been able to express the entire experiential cosmos in a musical form. Different scales are designed and employed for different times of the day, as well as for each month and season of the year. There are numerous *ragas* (traditional melodic patterns or modes) for every special event, celebration, and religious ritual. The entire palette of music has an evocative nature; it focuses energy on each experience, each moment of life.

Within this strict structure of scales and rhythmic patterns, the Indian musician is allowed ample opportunity to improvise. Thus, the personal experiences and fleeting moods of the artists are also integrated into the sounds.

The different tenor of each time of day is reflected in Western music as well, such as in Gregorian chant and hymnody. And in certain programmed pieces, such as Ferde Grofé's *Grand Canyon Suite,* the time of day, the season, and even the weather conditions of a place are clearly orchestrated. The movements of Vivaldi's *The Four Seasons* evoke the spirits of the different parts of the year, and are always popular among concertgoers. But in the case of these latter works, we've often missed the opportunity to fully experience each piece in its appropriate time and setting.

The spectrum of music's expressive power expands far beyond verbal descriptions such as "fast," "slow," "happy," and "sad." Words can never convey the vast range of emotions and physical sensation that we experience when we listen to it.

The Indian tradition of creating music for specific activities and for each part of the day can teach us new ways of using sound in our own world. By developing a "sonic clock," we can enhance our creativity and health— that is, by simply incorporating stimulating tunes into our day, we can pick up our spirits. At other times, we can select a piece that will calm us. Specific melodies can spur our mental processes, encourage daydreams and pleasant memories, or create an environment for spiritual insight. While most of us instinctively use music to create or enhance our moods now and then, we seldom consider how to consciously counteract the noise and stress around us by creating a diet for "sound" health.

Working with Your Cycles of Stress

Take a moment to examine one of your normal days during the week, and write your reflections on the following experiences:

- **Waking up each morning**
  - Are you relaxed and refreshed, or are you tired?
  - Do you want to stay in bed or begin your day?
  - Is there time for a calm first hour, or do you always feel rushed?
  - Are your muscles tense?

- **Lunchtime**
  - Do you have at least half an hour for a calm lunch?
  - Do you share your mealtime with others?
  - Do you feel rushed while eating?

- **Midafternoon**
  - Are you on a nonstop schedule, or do you take a break?
  - How often are you tired or bored?

- **Dinnertime**
  - Are you able to take a break after your afternoon activities?
  - Is there a transition period between work and dinner?
  - Do you look forward to your evening meal?
  - Is this time rushed or relaxed?

- **Evening**
  - Are you relaxed or tired at the end of the day?

- How many times do you make a conscious effort to unwind through exercise, meditation, or participating in the arts?
- Do you feel that you had time for yourself during the day?
- What have you noticed as you've experimented with the images and music in this book?
- Have you been able to be consistent in the time you spend with the exercises?

A cycle of stress can gradually build over time and create a great strain on our bodies. Often, the habits of stress become addictive as early as our student years. We seldom become aware of their damaging effects until much later, when the accumulated tension manifests itself emotionally, mentally, or physically.

There are a variety of reasons why we initially enter these cycles. Physical tension can be initiated by trauma, illness, intense labor, poor diet, and lack of exercise, while psychological strain may spring from many forms of worry, anger, shame, guilt, and conflicts with others. When we sense a lack of control in our lives, our stress level increases remarkably.

Psychosocial anxiety is created by difficulty in our relationships with family members, friends, or colleagues; while psychospiritual pressure results from challenges to our inner belief system, ethics, and values.

Some stress is actually good for us, since challenges, exercise, and deep contemplative thought can lead us to a more compassionate and healthy way of being. Yet when we prolong any deep pattern that exhausts us, our bodies begin to respond accordingly.

Try this exercise:

- While in bed, deeply inhale and imagine fresh bright light and energy coming into your body.

- Take a moment to tense your legs, and then relax as you exhale.

- Continue to breathe, and keep releasing the stress from your mind and shoulders with every exhalation.

- You may wish to play one of the selections from the CD and create your own affirmation to accompany this exercise.

Instead of attempting to deal with all of your stress in the last hours of your day, begin calming yourself first thing in the morning, take five minutes at noon, and then do another short relaxation exercise in the early evening. You'll find that the techniques in this book are quick and efficient ways to balance your mind and body throughout the day.

Often when we're learning to relax, we feel vulnerable or somewhat emotional. These activities and music are designed to slowly align the mind, emotions, and body for a healthy renewal of energy and sleep. Be patient, and allow a few weeks to integrate your experiences and wisdom.

Creating Your Own Relaxation Symphony

Dancing, moving, and being energized by music can serve as the perfect prelude to many of the techniques that have been presented in this book. As with the exercise that you tried in Chapter 2 (in which you tensed your muscles before relaxing), music that energizes you may allow for a deeper state of rest afterward.

Some mornings you may need sonic caffeine just to get out of bed! So, following these powerful sounds, perform the relaxation activity that you enjoy most, relaxing and stretching to music before and after. Become conscious of your body throughout the day, select music that expresses and enhances the mood of the moment . . . and then relax! Whether you see these exercises as mini tune-ups or musical meditations, create your times of harmony with consciousness and attentiveness. By exploring the many styles of music, images, and thoughts, you'll soon find what works best for you.

Health is about making the body sound; in fact, it comes from the Old English word *hal,* signifying "to be whole." In other words, it leads to balance and harmony, not perfection. You must allow your natural, relaxed instincts to usher the ease of being into your daily experience.

In this final exercise, you'll be able to take flight with some of the most beautiful music ever composed. "The Lark Ascending," one of the most popular classical pieces in the British repertoire, was written by Ralph Vaughan Williams during the First World War. The power of the melodious birdsong and the flow of flight inspired the musical images and colorful charm of his pastoral piece for solo violin and chamber orchestra. The result is scenic, harmonious, and rich with calm yet joyous emotion. Based on folk songs and inspired by a poem by George Meredith, the scenic ascent from the comfort and beauty of the earth toward heaven is gradual and inspiring. Here is an excerpt from Meredith's poem:

For singing 'til his heaven fills,
'Tis love of earth that he instills,
And ever winging up and up,
Our valley is his golden cup
And he the wine which overflows
To lift us with him as he goes. . . .
Till lost on his aerial rings
In light, and then the fancy sings.

Using Music, Visualization, and Affirmations for This Chapter

Step One

Affirmation:
I release tension with every breath,
allowing harmony and peace to abound.

- Close your eyes and imagine that you're gliding like a bird through fresh, calm air.

- Allow your body to surrender to the light and beauty of the sky and earth.

- Whether you're sitting or standing, allow your arms to extend as if you were a bird gliding to a brilliant star.

- Take a few minutes to repeat this affirmation: *I release tension with every breath, allowing harmony and peace to abound.*

Step Two

After the affirmation feels comfortable and spontaneous, open your eyes and look at the star at the end of this chapter.

- See if you can keep your eyes focused right on the center of the star as you inhale.

- As you exhale, add the affirmation, and imagine that you're floating toward the star. Do this five or six times as you keep your eyes focused on the shape.

- Close your eyes and rest in the thought and image. Notice whether you can still see the star with your inner vision.

Step Three

Now begin to play Track 5 of the enclosed CD; this piece is "The Lark Ascending," by Ralph Vaughan Williams.

- Listen to the selection once with your eyes closed in order to relax your body.

- Then play the music again as you look into the center of the star.

- Next, add this affirmation: *I release tension with every breath, allowing harmony and peace to abound.*

- Let this music lift you from tension and stress.

*I release tension
with every breath,
allowing harmony
and peace to abound.*

Music: Track 5, "The Lark Ascending,"
by Ralph Vaughan Williams

CD Track List

1. Michael Hoppé, "Beloved," 3:06

2. Gabriel Fauré; "Sicilienne, Op. 78"; Nora Shulman, flute; Judy Loman, harp; 3:42

3. Edvard Grieg; "Morning," from *Peer Gynt, Suite No. 1;* Nora Shulman, flute; Judy Loman, harp; 3:42

4. Wolfgang Amadeus Mozart; "Andante," from *Piano Concerto No. 14 in E Flat Major*; Jenö Jandó, piano; Concentus Hungaricus; András Ligeti, conductor; 6:36

5. Ralph Vaughan Williams; "The Lark Ascending"; David Greed, violin; English Northern Philharmonia; David Lloyd-Jones, conductor; 15:08

   Music licensed courtesy of Spring Hill Music LLC.

Suggested Reading

Healing Imagery and Music. Carol A. Bush. Portland, Oregon: Rudra Press, 1999.

Mind, Music and Imagery. Stephanie Merritt. Santa Rosa, California: Aslan Publishing, 1996.

The Mozart Effect®. Don Campbell. New York: HarperCollins, Inc., 2001.

Music and Soulmaking. Barbara Crowe. Lanham, Maryland: Scarecrow Press, 2004.

Music: Physician for Times to Come. Don Campbell. Wheaton, Illinois: Quest Books, 2000.

The Relaxation Response. Herbert Benson, M.D., with Miriam Z. Klipper. New York: HarperTorch, 2000.

Rituals of Healing: Using Imagery for Health and Wellness. Jeanne Achterberg, Ph.D.; Barbara Dossey, R.N.; and Leslie Kolkmeier, R.N. New York: Bantam Books, 1994.

Stress Management. James S. Gordon, M.D. New York: Chelsea House, 2000.

The Tao of Music. John M. Ortiz. York Beach, Maine: Samuel Weiser, Inc., 1997.

For more information on Don Campbell's books and CDs, as well as a vast guide to music, music therapy, education, and health:

The Mozart Effect Resource Center
800-721-2177
www.mozarteffect.com

For more information on Don Campbell's innovative work in health-care settings, contact:

Aesthetic Audio Systems
619-683-7512
www.aestheticas.net

Suggested Listening

Deep Listening. Pauline Oliveros. New Albion Records NA022

Eight String Religion. David Darling. Wind Over The Earth WE2320

Adagio. Compilation of Relaxing Classics. Naxos 8.550994

Floating World. Riley Lee and Marshall McGuire. New World Music 603

Inner Peace for Busy People: Music to Relax and Renew. Joan Borysenko. Spring Hill Music 6031.2

Largo. Compilation of Baroque Music. Naxos 8.550950

Music for The Mozart Effect®, Volume 5: Relax and Unwind. Don Campbell, Spring Hill Music 6505.2

Solace. Michael Hoppé. Spring Hill Music 6042.2

About the Author

Don Campbell is a recognized authority on the transformative power of music, listening, and The Mozart Effect®. He's a leading lecturer and consultant to health-care organizations, corporations, parenting groups, and more. He works with audiences of symphony orchestras on how music can affect learning, healing, and other aspects of our lives.

Don is the acoustic and musical director of Aesthetic Audio Systems, an innovative company that provides quality music to health-care facilities. His books have been translated into 20 languages, and he has lectured in more than 25 countries, including South Africa, Brazil, Poland, Ireland, India, Israel, and Japan. He has recently keynoted conferences for Yale University, The Royal Dublin Society, The Society for Arts in Healthcare, and The International Teachers Associations in Japan and South America. He presently serves on the board of the American Music Research Center at the University of Colorado.

Don serves on many national boards, including ARTS for People and the Duke University Medical School. In 2004, he was honored with the Distinguished Fellow award from the National Expressive Therapy Association. He has also been awarded "Director Emeritus" of the Boulder Philharmonic Orchestra. In Don's unique view, music is not only a rich and rewarding aesthetic experience, but an easily accessible bridge to a more creative, intelligent, healthy, and joy-filled life. His singular mission is to help return music to its central place in the modern world as a resource for growth, development, health, and celebration.

Don is the author of 17 books, including *Music: Physician for Times to Come, Rhythms of Learning,* and the 1997 bestseller *The Mozart Effect.* He has also produced 16 albums, including the accompanying music for the Mozart Effect series for adults and children, which dominated the classical *Billboard* charts in 1998 and 1999.

Acknowledgments

My deepest appreciation goes to Bill Horwedel at Spring Hill Music for his visionary practicality and friendship. Thanks to Reid Tracy, Jill Kramer, Jessica Vermooten, Christy Salinas, and Charles McStravick at Hay House for their skillful development of this book.

My sincere gratitude to Marianne Cenko and Sherill Tippins for their editing, proofing, and creative suggestions. Thanks also to Judith Cornell, Jeanne Achterberg, Hazel Lee, Ruby Nowland, and Michael Hoppé.

96

Hay House Titles of Related Interest

Books

Angel Medicine: *How to Heal the Body and Mind*
with the Help of the Angels,
by Doreen Virtue, Ph.D.

Getting in the Gap: *Making Conscious Contact*
with God Through Meditation (book-with-CD),
by Dr. Wayne W. Dyer

Heal Your Body, by Louise L. Hay

Inner Peace for Busy People,
by Joan Z. Borysenko, Ph.D.

Silent Power (book-with-CD), by Stuart Wilde

Sound Choices: *Using Music to Design the Environments*
in Which You Live, Work, and Heal,
by Susan Mazer and Dallas Smith

CDs

The Beginner's Guide to Meditation, by Joan Z. Borysenko, Ph.D.

Complete Relaxation, by Denise Linn

The Divine Name: *Sounds of the God Code,*
by Gregg Braden and Jonathan Goldman

All of the above are available at your local bookstore, or may be ordered by contacting:
Hay House USA: **www.hayhouse.com;** Hay House Australia: **www.hayhouse.com.au;**
Hay House UK: **www.hayhouse.co.uk;** Hay House South Africa: **orders@psdprom.co.za;**
Hay House India: **www.hayhouseindia.co.in**

♪

We hope you enjoyed this Hay House book.
If you'd like to receive a free catalog featuring additional
Hay House books and products, or if you'd like information about the
Hay Foundation, please contact:

Hay House, Inc.
P.O. Box 5100
Carlsbad, CA 92018-5100

(760) 431-7695 or **(800) 654-5126**
(760) 431-6948 (fax) or **(800) 650-5115 (fax)**
www.hayhouse.com® • **www.hayfoundation.org**

Published and distributed in Australia by: Hay House Australia Pty. Ltd. • 18/36 Ralph St. •
Alexandria NSW 2015 • *Phone:* 612-9669-4299 • *Fax:* 612-9669-4144 • www.hayhouse.com.au

Published and distributed in the United Kingdom by: Hay House UK, Ltd. •
Unit 62, Canalot Studios • 292 Kensal Rd., London W10 5BE • *Phone:* 44-20-8962-1230 •
Fax: 44-20-8962-1239 • www.hayhouse.co.uk

Published and distributed in the Republic of South Africa by: Hay House SA (Pty), Ltd.,
P.O. Box 990, Witkoppen 2068 • *Phone/Fax:* 27-11-706-6612 • orders@psdprom.co.za

Published in India by: Hay House Publications (India) Pvt. Ltd., 3 Hampton Court, A-Wing,
123 Wodehouse Rd., Colaba, Mumbai 400005 • *Phone:* 91 (22) 22150557 or 22180533 •
Fax: 91 (22) 22839619 • www.hayhouseindia.co.in

Distributed in India by: Media Star, 7 Vaswani Mansion, 120 Dinshaw Vachha Rd.,
Churchgate, Mumbai 400020 • *Phone:* 91 (22) 22815538-39-40 •
Fax: 91 (22) 22839619 • booksdivision@mediastar.co.in

Distributed in Canada by: Raincoast • 9050 Shaughnessy St., Vancouver, B.C. V6P 6E5 •
Phone: (604) 323-7100 • *Fax:* (604) 323-2600 • www.raincoast.com

Tune in to **HayHouseRadio.com®** for the best in inspirational talk radio featuring
top Hay House authors! And, sign up via the Hay House USA Website to receive the
Hay House online newsletter and stay informed about what's going on with your
favorite authors. You'll receive bimonthly announcements about: Discounts and
Offers, Special Events, Product Highlights, Free Excerpts, Giveaways, and more!
www.hayhouse.com®